FINDING YOUR TRUE LOVE

Learn How To Attract The Person Of Your Dreams

Jackson Moore

Table of Contents

PART 1

Chapter 1:

7 Signs You Have Found A Keeper

Are you looking for Mr. or Mrs. Right? Or do you think you have found the right person, but how can you be sure? Sometimes, we meet someone who seems like the person you would want to spend your whole life with, but during those times, someone is in for a quick hookup. The only partners worth keeping are the ones that give you the positive vibes that you need after a dull and tedious day, the ones that make you feel happy, and your relationship doesn't feel boring at all. Here are signs that you have found a keeper.

1. They inspire you to become a better person:

When we meet someone very kind, helpful and overall a friendly person that person usually inspires us to be better and luckily the world is full of friendly people. Is your partner like this too? Is he warm, kind, and helpful? Does he inspire you to become a better version of yourself? Then you know you have found yourself a keeper. You know you have found the right person when your partner works hard, gives you and his family time, and has his life organized.

2. They are always there:

There are times when we all suffer when things get tough to handle. At times like these, a person always needs support and love to get through the hard times. If your partner is there for you even when you can't defend yourself and they cheer you up, you know that this is a keeper. A perfect partner is someone who knows how to make you laugh even when you are crying, your partner will never believe the things people talk about behind your back, and he would never hesitate to lend you a hand when you need some help.

3. They know you more than yourself:

Sometimes it fascinates us how someone can know us more than we know ourselves; it feels perfect when someone knows how or what we are thinking. If your partner knows what you are feeling without telling them, then they are the one. Does your partner know what you are comfortable with? Can they tell when you feel upset? Do they motivate you to do better and ask you to chase after your dreams? If so, then don't waste more time thinking if this is the right person for you because it is.

4. Your interests are common:

Sure, opposites attract, but too many differences are not usually suitable for someone's relationship. It would help if you had a common interest with your partner, like having common beliefs, values, and religious perspectives. When you agree on these things, your bond will become more robust, and you would find it very easy to live with that person.

5.   They are honest with you:

Finding an honest person is a tiring thing to do; many people lie more than twice a day, but how can that affect your relationship? The right one may lie about small things that don't matter that much, like whether the color suits you or not; they may say those things to make you feel good about yourself, but lying about other things like financial status, health, or fidelity can be more serious. A true keeper would never keep these things from you, and they would always be honest with you even if the truth upsets you.

6.   They don't feel tired of you:

Although everyone needs some space, even from the person they love the most, he will never get tired of you if he is the one. Your partner will never feel bored with you; on the contrary, your partner will never get tired of looking at you, admiring you, being with you, and above all, love you. When a person is so in love with you that they want to spend every second of their life with you, then you know you have found a keeper.

7.   You are a part of their dreams:

Can your partner not even imagine your life without you? Has your partner already planned his future, and you are a big part of it? If so, you know that this one's a keeper. You both have reached a point in your lives where even thinking about living without each other sounds absurd, and then you know that you have found a keeper.

Conclusion:

A keeper is someone that loves, cherishes, and cares for you like no one has ever had. Don't worry if you haven't found your keeper, and it is just a matter of time before you do because, for every one of us, there is someone out there.

Chapter 2:
Ten Ways Men Fall In Love

Genuine and true Love is so rare that when you encounter it in any form, it's a beautiful thing to be utterly cherished in whatever form it takes. But how does one get this genuine and true Love? Almost every romantic movie, we have seen that a guy meets a girl and, sure enough, falls head over heels for her. But translating that into the real world can be quite a task. The science of attraction works wonders for us. Sometimes we are instantly drawn to some people. On the other hand, we couldn't care less for others. And quite a few times, things flow naturally in our direction, making it all feel surreal and causing butterflies.

A famous psychologist once said: "Love is about an expansion of the self whereby another person's interests, values, social network, and finances become part of your life just as you share your resources with them."

A human mind is, nonetheless, a very complex organ. It can either makes you feel like you're on top of the world with its positive attitude or under it with its negative one. And a male mind, perhaps, seems always like a mystery to us. But it's not such rocket science that we can't get our hands on it. If you're developing feelings for someone and need a bit of guidance to get the man of your dreams to notice you and care about you, then you've just come to the right place!

Here are some ways about what a man needs to fall in Love.

1. Always Be Yourself:

Keeping a façade of fake personality and pretending to be someone you're not can be a huge turn-off for men. Instead let the guy know the real you. Let them see who you really are and what you really have to offer. You will not only gain respect from them, but you wouldn't have to keep hiding behind a mask. If you're pretending to be someone else, that only suggests that you're not comfortable with yourself. And many guys will realize this shortcoming and quickly become disinterested. You don't have to dumb down your intellect or put a damper on your exuberant personality. Men like women who are completely honest with them from the start. Who shows them their vulnerable side as well as their opinionated and intelligent one. You're in no need to pretend that your IQ isn't off the charts. Be your genuine, miserable, confident, and independent self always. That way, he will know exactly what he's getting into.

2. Make him feel accepted and appreciated:

From a simple thank you text to calling him and asking him about his day, making small gestures for him, and complimenting and praising him, a man needs it all. Men don't always show it, but they are loved to be told that they look good, they're doing a good job, or how intellectual they are. Sometimes men are confused about where women may stand, and they want to see that he's being supported beyond any superficial matter.

When men share glimpses of their inner self with you and put themselves in a vulnerable position, which men rarely do, this is when it's crucial to make him feel rest assured that he will be accepted and appreciated. If women make men feel lifted high and admired, then it's pure magic for them. His heart will make such a deep connection with you that it can only be amplified from thereon.

3. Listen! Don't just talk:

You would see a lot of men complain that they are not heard enough. And quite frankly, it is true. It's essential to establish a mutual balance in the conversation. Women shouldn't make it all about themselves. They need to let the men speak and hear them attentively, and respond accordingly. Ask him questions about his life and his passion, his likes and dislikes. That way, he'll know that you are genuinely interested in him. Men have a lot to say when you show that you can listen. They'll be more inclined to say the things that matter.

4. Laugh out loud with him:

Men tend to make the women of their liking laugh a lot. When you're laughing, you're setting off chemicals in a guy's brain to feel good. Make him feel like he has a great sense of humor, and he's making you happy with his silly and jolly mannerism. Similarly, men are attracted to women who have a spirit that can make them feel good. Tell him enjoyable stories, roast people with him, jump in on his jokes and laugh wholeheartedly with him. He will become attracted to you.

5.   Look your best:

You don't have to shred a few pounds, or get clear, glowing skin, or change your hairstyle to impress the men of your liking. You have to be confident enough in your skin! Men love a confident woman who feels secure about herself and her appearance. You don't even have to wear body-hugging clothes or tight jeans to make him drool over you (Of course, you can wear them if you want). But a simple pair of jeans and a t-shirt can go a long way too. Just remember to clean yourself up nice, put on nice simple clothes, wear that unique perfume, style up your hair a bit, and voila! You're good to go.

6.   Be trustworthy:

Another reason that men instantly attract you is when they have the surety that they can trust you with anything and everything. According to love and marriage experts "Trust is not something all loving relationships start with, but successful marriages and relationships thrive on it. Trust is so pervasive that it becomes part of the fabric of these strong relationship." If you want to win a man's heart, reassure him that he can be vulnerable around you and make him feel accepted and secure.

7.   Don't try to change him:

"He's completely right for me... if only he didn't dress up like that or snore during his sleep."

Sure we might have a few things on our list about how our partner should be, but that doesn't mean we should forcibly try to change their habits. He might have a few annoying habits that will get on your nerves now and then, but that shouldn't be a dealbreaker for you. Instead, we should accept him with all his wits and flaws. You shouldn't just tolerate his little quirks but rather try to admire them too. If something about him is bothering you, try talking to him politely about it. And he might consider changing it for you!

8. Have intellectual conversations with him:

There's nothing that a man finds sexier than women with opinion and intellect. Get his views on a news article, engage him in a heated debate about controversial topics, put your views out the front; even if they clash with his, especially if they conflict with his, he'd be more interested and intrigued about knowing your stance. Show your future partner that you can carry on an intelligent conversation with him anytime he likes.

9. Be patient:

I can't stress enough that patience is perhaps the most vital key to getting a guy to fall for you. It would be best if you gave him time to analyze and process his feelings for you. If you tend to rush him on the subject, you might end up disappointed. Even if you do lose your cool, don't let him know it. Just be patient and consistent, and don't come off as too clingy or needy. If you appear too desperate, it's going to turn him off of the relationship entirely.

10. **Let him know you're thinking of him:**

In the early days of dating, you might be hesitant to tell him that you're thinking of him. You love it when he texts you randomly, saying he's thinking about you, so why not reciprocate it? Invest your time, energy, and efforts in him. Leave him short, sweet notes, or text him in the middle of the day saying that he is on your mind or sending him a greeting card with a cute personal message. Don't overdo it by reminding him constantly if he does not respond. None of these screams' overboard' and are guaranteed to make him smile.

Conclusion:

I hope this article deconstructed and gave you some insights into what makes a man fall for a woman. As the saying goes, 'Men are from mars and women are from Venus and Venus is great, but surely, we need to know about the inner workings of mars too.' Just keep the above tips in mind, be consistent and commit to him considerably, and you're good to go! If you found this video helpful, don't forget to like, subscribe, comment, and share this with someone important to you. I hope you learned something valuable today. Take care, have a good rest, and till the next video ☺

1.

Chapter 3:

8 Signs A Girl Likes You

The human mind is considered one of the most complicated organs, and understanding the female mind can be a hell of a task. In 2017, a professor of neurobiology and behaviour, Larry Cahill, Ph.D., issued the differences between a male and a female mind in his research The Journal of neuroscience. He says that although the total brain size of men is more extensive than women, but a woman's hippocampus, critical to learning and memorization, is more significant than a man's and works differently. The two hemispheres of a woman's brain talk to each other more than a man's do.

Women are fascinating, inspiring, and quite complex creatures. And if you're unsure about the signs that a girl might like you, then you're in it for the long run. Mostly, men are expected to make the first move, like approaching a girl, striking up a conversation, or simply asking a girl out on a date. But women play the lead role in deciding whether a man can initiate romantic advances. They initiate the contact by subtly providing cues if the communication is welcome or not.

It's difficult to decipher a woman's behavior, especially if she's giving you mixed signals. But worry not! we're here to help you see the signs clearly of whether a girl likes you or not. So, save yourself some stress, put your decoder ring on, and let's get started.

Here are 8 signs to know if a girl likes you...

1. She makes eye contact and holds it.

While a lot of people shies away when making eye contact, if you see a girl holding it for more than a fraction of a second (3-5 seconds max), then there's a strong possibility that she's into you. Research says that when you see something that your brain likes, it releases oxytocin and dopamine into your system. These hormones make you feel incredibly joyous. Notice her eyes the next time she makes eye contact with you; if her pupils dilate, then she's definitely interested in you.

2. She laughs at all your jokes (even the lame ones).

When a woman notices a man she's interested in, she would smile, laugh, and giggle more often around him. Even if your jokes are terrible (everyone agrees), but this girl would act as if you're the funniest guy she's ever met. If she counterattacks you with the same humorous and playful banter instead of getting offended, then she's really interested in you. Relationship expert Kate Spring says humor is a sure-fire sign of confidence. And confidence sparks something deep inside women that sets off instant attraction.

3. She mirrors your behavior.

A study published in the Personality and Social Psychology Bulletin proved that subtle "behavioral mimicry" indicates that you're attracted to that person. You might notice that she has adopted your slang, the way that you move your hands while making a conversation, or the pace at which you talk. Jane McGonigal, researcher and author of The New York Times bestseller "Reality is Broken", calls mirroring a love detector. She says, "….the more we feel like we really understand somebody, we're really connecting with them, we're really really clicking with them, the more likely we are to mirror what they're doing physically."

4. She makes frequent contact with you.

Instigating conversations can be a lot of hard work for a woman since they expect the opposite gender to start the chit-chat. So, if she's constantly engaging in discussions with you, making efforts by replying to you properly, and getting to know you better, she certainly likes you. Relationship expert Dresean Ryan says, "Believe it or not, something as simple as a good morning text can show someone has deep feelings for you."

5. She touches you.

One of the most obvious signs that she's into you is when she touches you. It could be a light brush of her hand against yours, slapping your shoulder playfully, or touching your leg or hair. If she's initiating the touch and does not creep out by yours, instead she seems comfortable with you, then it's a great sign of her being interested in you. According to behavior analyst Jack Schafer, "women may lightly touch the arm of the person they are talking to. This light touch is not an invitation to a sexual encounter; it merely indicates that she likes you."

6. She gets nervous around you.

If you're around and she seems to become quiet all of a sudden or starts avoiding you, then know that she's nervous and not uninterested. She might start playing with her hair, rubbing her hands, interlacing her fingers, blink frequently, or compress her lips. If you also notice that her breathing has become ragged and fast when you've entered the room, then that's a lucky sign for you.

7. She's always available for you.

Whether you're in a middle of an existential crisis at 3 in the morning or simply want to go for lunch, you text her, and she's at your door the minute after. Even if she's busy, she'll move things around her schedule just to fit you in. You can easily tell by her body language and her behaviors that she loves spending time with you. She's always there for you whenever you need something, going through a bad phase, or enjoying life.

8. Her friends know about you.

Women tell their friends everything. And by everything, I mean every single thing. So, if she's confident enough to introduce you to her friends, then consider yourself lucky. If they tease her when you're around or start praising her more in front of you, then there's definitely more to the matter. The approval of family and friends is the most critical aspect in seeing whether the individual cares enough to see a future with you.

Conclusion:

Figuring out if a woman likes you is a very tricky business. You might get silences or mixed signals in the initial few days. But it would be best if you looked for the social cues that women give off when they're attracted to you. Try your best and do not give up, you'll eventually get her!

Chapter 4:

6 Tips To Have A Healthy Long Distance Relationship

Who says long-distance relationships don't last? Well, a lot of your friends and family members would be against it, they would discourage it, and will advise you not to take it too seriously as for them, it'll only lead to your heartbreak. Honestly, it's not going to be easy. Long-distance would make most of the things unachievable, it could get complicated at times, and you will find yourself vulnerable, sad, and lonely. However, that extra distance also plays a role in getting both of you closer. Studies have found that long-distance relationships don't differ significantly from geographically close relationships, and even in some cases, it might even be better.

First of all, you should be comforted in knowing that long-distance relationships can succeed. With that in mind, we have combined a list of tips that will keep your long-distance relationship healthy and ensure that it lasts.

Technology Is Your Best Friend

In this age of facetime-ing and texting without paying sky-high rates, long-distance relationships are now easier than ever. You can share the day-to-day minutia with your partner by instantaneously sharing photos, exchanging texts and calls, and skyping one another. It'sIt's much different than writing a letter to your loved one and waiting weeks or months for a response. People in long-distance relationships also rely more heavily on technology to stay connected with each other. This helps them communicate verbally even more than the couples who see each other often, sit in the same room, and do not interact at all. It's essential not just to generalize but to share details with your partner. It would make both of you feel like you've witnessed each other's day.

Be Commited to The Relationship

This implies to everyone involved in relationships, but especially to people who are pursuing long-distance relationships. It's crucial to know that you're committed to only one person and that you love them before wasting your time as well as theirs. If you're choosing to stay in a long-distance relationship, you both must sort out where you both stand in life, what will happen next in your relationship, and that you both work towards a goal. It can be daunting to plan your future around another person, but it can do wonders for you both if we both work it through. Be vocal about your feelings so that the other person doesn't live in darkness about what you want.

Set An End Date

While long-distance love can be magical, but it's only a great thing for a finite time. Eventually, you would crave wanting to be in the same place as your partner. It can be hard to stay apart for a long time. One thing that'll help couples in this drastic time is to schedule a meeting and look forward to it every day. Both must stay equally committed to the relationship and should be on the same page about how long this situation would last. You and your partner's plans should align in eventually living in the same place.

Do Stuff Together, Even Though You're Apart

If you aren't physically in the same place, it doesn't mean you both can't have fun together. You can plan a movie night via skype or cook something together while facetime-ing each other. There are loads of streaming services available that make it easier to binge-watch your favorite shows with your partner. Apart from that, you can also search for some quizzes or games online that will connect both of you and help you find more about each other. You can also raise controversial topics and spark new and exciting conversations to see your partner's stance.

Make Fun Plans For When You Both Will Meet

Indulge into details of what the two of you will do the next time you see each other. Make it a ritual of discussing all of the stuff with your partner that you so eagerly look forward to doing with them. Be it trying new restaurants every day, or picking up a holiday destination, or simply choosing a new hobby to do together. You can also schedule good night video calls in your PJs to create a sense of you going to bed together.

Set Clear Rules and Boundaries

Don'tDon't do anything that you wouldn't expect your partner to do either. Try your best to stay out of situations that might make your partner feel insecure or uncomfortable. You don't have to check in with your partner for every approval, but you should set clear boundaries for the both of you and adhere to them.

Conclusion

It can get lonely and difficult sometimes when dealing with long-distance but know that the fruits, in the end, will be as sweet as heaven. Constantly inject positive energy into your relationship to keep it alive. Be grateful for your partner and be thankful for the fact that there's someone who loves you and whom you love.

Chapter 5:

7 Ways To Deal With An Overly Jealous Partner

Being jealous in a relationship seems cute at first, but it can really kill the love you and your partner have for each other after a while. You'll probably start to see the negative aspects of over jealousy pretty clearly. Some people have bad experiences and trust issues due to their past relationships, so being in a relationship with a jealous person shouldn't necessarily be a deal-breaker. It can be started by finding why your partner is feeling the way they feel, especially when you haven't given them a reason to mistrust you in the first place.

If your partner is being aggressive and trying to control what you're doing, you might want to try to work together with them to fix the issue. It will give them the reassurance they need and create a closer bond between you two. If your partner is turning red with jealousy lately, here are some signs for you to deal with them.

1. **Talk About Their Fears and Anxieties**

It would be best to calmly sit your partner down with you and ask them what's going on in their mind if you feel like your partner's jealousy is getting off the hook. Make sure you're listening to them fully attentively, and don't be scared to express how their thoughts affect you. Danielle B. Grossman, a California licensed marriage and family therapist, says, "Do not try to minimize, negate or 'fix' the fears. Do not try to bully your partner's fear into submission. Do not belittle, humiliate, shame, and threaten the fear." Always be empathetic and give them your undivided attention. Make sure you never attack your partner and make them trust that they can confide in you.

2. Don't Get Defensive About Your Behavior

If your partner is accusing you of something that is far from true, do not feed the fire by jumping right away into an argument. Evaluate the situation first. If you instantly try to get defensive, your partner will misinterpret your reaction or may get even angrier. Try to be patient first and deal with the situation calmly. Reassure them that whatever they're thinking isn't right, and you're always going to be with them no matter what.

3. Be Extra Affectionate

After discussing the reasons for their jealousy, show your partner extra love, during this weak and vulnerable time. This is the time to be more generous with your affection. Try to touch them more, make small gestures for them, and be supportive throughout this time. Of course, this means that you should take the abuse if extremely unhealthy jealousy is present. Don't let them force you into situations that you are uncomfortable dealing with.

4. Create Boundaries

Setting boundaries in your relationship isn't a negative thing at all. Loads of people in healthy relationships create a line to understand each other's emotions and priorities better. People should be aware of their selves even within a relationship. According to a Ph.D. psychologist Leslie Becker-Phelps, "You need to know what you like and dislike, what you're comfortable with versus what scares you, and how you want to be treated in the given situations." So, try your best not to let your mental health affect by your partner's conflicts.

5. Be Available and Responsive:

Although this issue is something that your partner needs to fix on their own, it can still help the situation get better if you're responsive when they reach out to you. If you're there when your partner needs you the most, and you tend to comfort them, it can help calm their jealous habits. This takes a lot of effort, without a doubt, but if your partner notices that you're available and receptive, then the trust between you two will only grow stronger with time.

6. Revisit The Issue and Be Patient

Over jealousy is an issue that can't be fixed overnight. You must be patient with your partner and show them now and then that you're willing to work on this problem together by supporting and discussing their fears. It can indeed be time-consuming and emotionally draining, but don't let it stop you from trying to work things out with your partner. Take baby steps, celebrate small victories until it isn't an issue anymore.

7. **Rebuild Your Trust**

If your partner is losing trust in you, make sure you gain it back by doing small things, such as facetiming them and texting them throughout the day, explaining to them why you're running late, or taking a rain check in advance if you know you're busy that day. Reassure them with positive statements, and this will eventually put your partner's fears at ease.

Conclusion

There's no magic spell or easy way to deal with a jealous partner, but if you want to make the relationship work, then put effort into it. Get your partner to trust you, be empathetic with them and talk about their feelings. This little bump in the road can probably go away, which will help you in the long run.

Chapter 6:

8 Signs You Have Found Your Soulmate

"People think a soulmate is your perfect fit, and that's what everyone wants. But a true soulmate is a mirror, the person who shows you everything that is holding you back, the person who brings you to your attention so you can change your life." - Elizabeth Gilbert.

Legends say that even before you were born, the name of your spiritual half was determined. The two souls roam around the world to find their significant other. Whenever they find one another, they will unite, and their spirits would become one. But finding our long-lost soulmate isn't as easy as we think it is. Out of 7 billion people, it could take some time to find out our perfect match. However, when we meet them, we'll click with them instantly and just know in our hearts that they are made for us. A soulmate is someone you keep coming back to, no matter the struggles, challenges, obstacles, downfalls, or any of the circumstances. Everything would feel perfect with them. But how do you know if someone is your soulmate? You needn't worry! We have compiled for you below the signs that you may have found your soulmate.

1. **They would bring the best in you:**

Have your friends called you boring or a party pooper since you have entered adult life? Of course, you blame it all on the fact that you have grown up now and have responsibilities. But there's this one person who tends to bring out the fun and sassy side of yours. You feel so comfortable around them that you're even willing to try new things with them. They make your anxiety and fear go away in the blink of an eye. Be it singing songs loudly in the crowd, trying bungee jumping, or just packing up your bags and moving across the country with them to pursue your goals and dreams, they will strengthen you by supporting your decisions and being there for you.

2. They won't play games with you:

They won't be inconsistent with you, like making you feel special one day and ignoring you completely the next. You won't be questioning his feelings about you or putting yourself in a state of over-thinking. Sure, they won't make grand gestures like showing up at your window holding a guitar at 3 in the morning or putting up a billboard saying how much they love you (although we will happily accept both). Still, they will make you realize your worth in their life by always prioritizing you, making you happy, asking about you throughout the day, and paying close attention to whatever you say.

3. You respect each other's differences:

When starting a new relationship, people tend to avoid or hold back specific thoughts, beliefs, or opinions. This is because, in the game of love, both of the couple's emotions are at stake. They don't speak their mind until and unless they're entirely comfortable with their partner. Your soulmate would always be open to change and respect your opinions and views, even if they disagree. They wouldn't ever implement their beliefs and ideas on you but would instead find comfort in knowing that you both don't have the same set of minds. It's essential to be on the same page with your partner on certain things, like the future, life goals, children, etc., but it's okay to have different moral and political views, as long as you both respect each other and it doesn't hurt the other's sentiments.

4. You forgive each other:

Being soulmates doesn't save you from the wrath of arguments and fights. Every relationship experiences indifference and frustration from time to time. But it is one of the things that makes your bond stronger with your partner. You both would rather sit and try to talk it through or sort it out instead of going to bed angry at each other. And when it comes to forgiving the other, you both would do it in a heartbeat. You wouldn't consider holding the other person guilty and would make unique gestures to try and make it up with them.

5. You give each other space:

Your partner doesn't constantly bug you by texting and calling you every minute. They don't ask you about your whereabouts and don't act overly possessive. And rightly so, you do the same with them. You give each other your space and know that the other person would always be there for you. Even if you have to ask them about some distance, they respect it without complaining. You both trust each other with your whole heart and respect them enough to give them the space they have asked for.

6. You empathize with each other:

If your soulmate tells you about them getting good grades in college, finding their dream job, or getting a promotion, you find yourself being more excited and happier for them than they are. Sometimes, we feel drained out by showing too much empathy to other people and understanding and friendly. But with your soulmate, you don't have to force it out or pretend, and it just comes naturally. Whenever they feel scared or anxious, you're right there with them, protecting them from the world and not leaving their side until you make sure they're okay.

7. You communicate with each other effectively:

They say that communication is essential for any long-lasting relationship. If you aren't communicating well with your partner, you might find yourself in the depths of overthinking the worst-case scenarios. Your partner makes it easy for you to share with them, even if you hadn't done the deed before. You find yourself talking about the tough things, the things that bother you or hurt you, and they comfort and console you reassure you that they will fix it. Similarly, you make sure your partner speaks your mind to you, and you do your best to right your wrongs and clear any of their doubts.

8. You have seen each other's flaws and still loves each other the same:

It isn't easy to accept someone with the habits or traits that you despise. However, you have been your complete and utter authentic version of yourself with them, and they still love you the same. Be it crying loudly while watching an emotional sitcom, binge eating at night, snoring, burping, or just showing them your weak and vulnerable phase when you tend to push everyone away and dress up like a homeless drug addict. They find your quirks cute and accept you with all your imperfections and flaws, and you do the same with them.

Conclusion:

A soulmate is someone who makes you realize your worth and brings out the best in you. They might drive you crazy, ignites your triggers, stirs your passions, but they might also be your most excellent teacher. They would allow you to discover your true self while always being there for you and supporting you all the way.

Chapter 7:

8 Signs That Someone Is Not Your Soulmate

When you find yourself in a relationship, everything feels fantastic. There are confused feelings everywhere, but those confusing feelings are just for the beginning. But we all do wonder if we'll ever find " the one." When we first enter a relationship, you may wonder if this is your soulmate. But sometimes, we want that one person to be our soulmate, but things just aren't meant to be that way. Here are a few signs that someone is not your soulmate.

1. It is tough to trust them:

If you feel yourself constantly spying about the whereabouts and motives of your partner because you feel like your partner is not honest with you, then you know that this person is not your soulmate. The reason behind this is that you can't just spend your whole life on the lookout. When you can't trust your soulmate no matter how much you try, you know that your partner is doing some shady stuff. A soulmate will be honest with their relationship even when you are not around because we all know, " Without trust, there is no relationship."

2. You don't connect at an emotional level:

In a relationship, you need to know all about your partner, about his life, his work, his future ambitions because if your connection with your partner is just surface level and you don't know anything about them, then you know that is not the "one." A soulmate would want to dig deeper into your soul and would want to know everything about you. Still, if you feel like they are not investing in the relationship and are not working for it, you may think that they are not interested in you or your life like a soulmate should be.

3. Your partner has different values than you:

Everyone has different values and meanings of life, but are these values too much further in your relationship? If so, then you know, this is not your soulmate. Indeed, a relationship requires compromise, but nobody can sacrifice too much, and having different values may as well result in that. Soulmates would have an essential, shared vision for the future.

4. He doesn't enhance your life:

A soulmate is someone who shows you a better side of yourself and life. A soulmate will make you feel complete, make you feel happy when you feel low, and give you the confidence you need. But if your partner makes no effort to help your personal growth or at least make you feel happy in your hard times, then you know that that is not your soulmate.

5. You wish to explore other interests:

It is entirely normal for a person that is in a relationship to find someone else attractive; after all, we all are human beings, but if you start picturing yourself with someone else and start wishing that you were single so you could explore other interests, then that is a huge sign you need to consider. When you find your soulmate, you would not wish to be single, and although other people still seem attractive, you would not want to leave your partner for them.

6. Your partner judges you:

All human beings have different views on life. Everybody thinks differently; indeed, there are things you and your partner do not have legal opinions on, and that is completely fine unless your partner starts judging you for doing something they don't like. Yes, a relationship does need compromise, but that surely does not mean that your partner gets the right to judge you because you did not compromise and still did something they don't like. A soulmate would never consider you for anything you do; a soulmate will understand you in the best possible way.

7. You don't feel the urge to text back:

Everybody knows that when you like someone, you reply to their messages as soon as you can. It is like a human being not to seem rude to the people they like, but if you don't want to reply to your partner, are you sure they are "the one"? If every other text you receive bothers you, and you don't feel that interested in them, you know that this person is not the one you were looking for.

8. **You don't just feel like telling him something important you:**

When you find the one, you want to tell them everything about yourself, including the essential things. But do you feel that way about your partner like you want to say everything about every day, or you just don't bother to tell? If you don't, then you know that he is not the one.

Conclusion:

Don't feel disheartened if you haven't found the right one yet because someone is made especially for you, and one day you will find your soulmate.

Chapter 8:

8 Signs Your Partner Is Cheating On You

One of the most traumatic and challenging experiences that a relationship might face is infidelity. Did you ever find yourself in a relationship that was going great but then suddenly, things started to change? You might be getting hindsight that your partner is cheating on you. But accusing your partner without any proof and making assumptions could take you in a bitter position more than him. A relationship coach with a Ph.D. in sociology, Marie Murphy, says, "There are no definitive, across-the-board, tell-tale signs of cheating unless you catch your partner red-handed, or they own up to what's going on."

And rightly so, you would give up on your suspicions most of the time because the cheating partners are extremely good at covering their tracks. Sometimes people change their behavior out of nowhere and without any reasonable explanation of what might have caused these changes. If they seem suspicious, it doesn't exactly add up to them being unfaithful. But some signs might suggest something is up. Some changes can be more telling than others. Below are some signs that will help you conclude if your suspicions were correct or you were merely overthinking.

1. **They're either constantly glued to their phone, or it's nowhere to be found:**

One of the significant signs of cheating, as the experts say, is their weird phone behavior. If you see them suddenly being on their phone all the time, even if they are with you, and they don't seem to share whatever they're doing or who they're talking to, then it may be a sign they're unfaithful to you. If you see them constantly blushing or smiling at their phones, be alert. You should pay extra attention if they're sticking their phone with them all the time because they just might be making sure you wouldn't see anything that they're hiding. In contrast, if you see them using their phone in your absence or tugging it away as soon as you arrive, it just could be another sign of infidelity.

2. **They have started to improve their appearance:**

Has your partner always avoided you when you lectured them about fitness, be lazy on the couch all day instead of hitting the gym, or would you always prefer eating junk over healthy? But you've noticed a few changes in your partner. They have started to get concerned about their body, their hairstyle, even their outfits. You get to see them hitting the gym every day and making six-packs, suddenly eating healthy, buying new jeans and shirts. They have started to wear their favorite perfume all day that they wouldn't even touch except for special occasions. All of these signs might indicate that your partner has found someone new whom they're trying to impress.

3.   Unexplained expenses:

If you see massive amounts of money being withdrawn from your partner's account without any trace of where exactly the money is going, then maybe your partner would be cheating on you. The costs of infidelity can add up very quickly because your partner might be paying for gifts, trips, dinners and hotel rooms, etc. You also notice unexplainable charges on credit card statements. And if you confront your partner about these expenses, the answer is usually untrue, or he just might avoid the question overall.

4.   They are usually angry and nervous around you:

If your partner has started to become frustrated and angry with you, even with little things, then it's likely that they are projecting their insecurities and fear on you. Your partner might have a sudden change in their moods and emotions. The partner you once recognized as the most humorous and jolly person in the room has become grumpy and weird. You find your partner getting mad at you about stuff that doesn't even make sense. According to Lillian Glass, a Ph.D., "You can tell that your partner is hiding something if they rock back and forth while chatting with you." This indicates nervousness.

5.   Their schedule suddenly changes:

If your partner is preparing unplanned trips all of a sudden, taking days off from work, and tells you at the very last minute without asking you to come along, then it may be a sign of your partner cheating on you.

Especially if they're going with a work colleague and brushes you off the moment, they get there by saying they're busy attending a bunch of work meetings, and then you might consider looking into the matter. A psychologist Paul Coleman suggests, "Someone who must work late all of a sudden at times that go beyond a reasonable explanation may be cheating."

6. Their friends are acting weird all of a sudden:

Friends are the most important people in one's life. They almost know about everything that you're dealing with. And chances are, your partner's friends might know about them cheating on you long before you do. So if you're suspicious about your partner's activities, confront their friends. If their friends seem odd or nervous around you or can't look you in the eye, then definitely something's up.

7. There's a change in communication:

Suppose you and your partner discuss even the tiniest things and sort out any argument right away. Still, suddenly your partner has become distant, and you don't share the same level of communication anymore. In that case, there might be a problem. You might notice some changes, such as your partner completely ignores whatever you say, acts in a passive-aggressive manner, refuses to answer any of your questions, makes accusations, or storms off without saying a word. All these could be signs of infidelity as your partner has found someone else to rely on and shares all of their problems with someone else now.

8. They're suddenly extremely affectionate towards you:

This may sound a bit odd, but it can be a clear sign if you think hard enough. Your partner may suddenly shower you with praises and adoration to manipulate you in the future. They would do anything in their power to keep you happy, so you might now question if they're cheating on you or not. Another reason can be that they feel so guilty about cheating on you that they may and try to 'make up for it.' You might think that your partner is making you feel extra special, buying you your favorite things, and making you your favorite foods, all more than expected. This might be a sign of danger.

Conclusion:

You must consider all the above signs if you're suspicious about your partner cheating on you. However, your partner may indicate all these signs and still could not be cheating on you. So first, make sure by doing all of your detective work and then come to any conclusion.

Chapter 9:

6 Signs You Have A Fear of Intimacy

Intimacy avoidance or avoidance anxiety, also sometimes referred to as the fear of intimacy, is characterized as the fear of sharing a close emotional or physical relationship with someone. People who experience it do not consciously want to avoid intimacy; they even long for closeness, but they frequently push others away and may even sabotage relationships for many reasons.

The fear of intimacy is separate from the fear of vulnerability, though both of them can be closely intertwined. A person who has a fear of intimacy may be comfortable becoming vulnerable and showing their true self to their trusted friends and relatives. This problem often begins when a person finds relationships becoming too close or intimate. Fear of intimacy can stem from several causes. Overcoming this fear and anxiety can take time, but you can work on it if you know the signs of why you have the fear in the first place.

1. Fear Of Commitment

A person who has a fear of intimacy can interact well with others initially. It's when the relationship and its value grow closer that everything starts to fall apart. Instead of connecting with your partner on an intimate level, you find ways and excuses to end the relationship and replace it with yet another superficial relationship. Some might even call you a 'serial dater,' as you tend to lose interest after a few dates and abruptly end the relationship. The pattern of emerging short-term relationships and having a 'commitment phobia' can signify that you fear intimacy.

2. Perfectionism

The idea of perfectionism often works to push others away rather than draw them near. The underlying fear of intimacy often lies in a person who thinks he does not deserve to be loved and supported. The constant need for someone to prove themself to be perfect and lovable can cause people to drift apart from them. Absolute perfectionism lies in being imperfect. We should be able to accept the flaws of others and should expect them to do the same for us. There's no beauty in trying to be perfect when we know we cannot achieve it.

3. Difficulty Expressing Needs

A person who has a fear of intimacy may have significant difficulty in expressing needs and wishes. This may stem from feeling undeserving of another's support. You need to understand that people cannot simply 'mind read,' they cannot know your needs by just looking at you; this might cause you to think that your needs go unfulfilled and your feelings of unworthiness are confirmed. This can lead to a vicious cycle of you not being vocal about your needs and lacking trust in your partner, and your relationship is meant to doom sooner or later.

4. Sabotaging Relationships

People who have a fear of intimacy may sabotage their relationship in many ways. You might get insecure, act suspicious, and accuse your partner of something that hasn't actually occurred. It can also take the form of nitpicking and being very critical of a partner. Your trust in your partner would lack day by day, and you would find yourself drifting apart from them.

5. Difficulties with Physical Contact

Fear of intimacy can lead to extremes when it comes to physical contact. It would swing between having a constant need for physical contact or avoiding it entirely. You might be inattentive to your partner's needs and solely concentrate on your own need for sexual release or gratification. People with a fear of intimacy may also recoil from sex altogether. Both ends of the spectrum lead to an inability to let go or communicate intimately emotionally. Letting yourself be emotionally naked and bringing up your fears and insecurities to your partner may help you overcome this problem.

6. You're Angry - A Lot

One way that the deep, subconscious fear of intimacy can manifest is via anger. Constant explosions of anger might indicate immaturity, and immature people are not able to form intimate relationships. Everyone gets angry sometimes, and it's an emotion that we cannot ignore, even if we want to. But if you find that your feelings of anger bubble up constantly or inappropriately, a fear of intimacy may be lurking underneath. Don't deny these intimacy issues, but instead put them on the table and communicate effectively with the person you are interested in.

Conclusion

Actions that root out in fear of intimacy only perpetuate the concern. With effort, especially a good therapist, many people have overcome this fear and developed the understanding and tools needed to create a long-term intimate relationship.

PART 2

Chapter 1:

6 Steps To Recover From A Breakup

Breakups are tough to go through. Even when they end with good terms, it still brings out many insecurities and traumas of the past. These include the fear of abandonment, loneliness, etc. Breakups have become a prevalent thing for us, so familiar that we sometimes forget how painful it can be. When you have imagined your whole future with someone, and someone ends up leaving you, you feel broken, but you would know it happened for a reason. Recovering from a breakup is not an impossible thing to do, and most of us recover from a partition even if it may take some time. Here are a few steps to recover from a breakup.

1. Talk About It

After a breakup, everything seems to be falling apart, and it is tough to talk about it, about the pain it has caused. But it is scientifically proven that talking about your breakup helps you recover from it; as you start talking about it, you are reminded about what went wrong. This enables you to understand that it was for good. When you talk about it to others, they tell you their perspective, and you start to see things from a different point of view; this way, you understand what went wrong, and you begin to feel more okay with things.

2. Keep A Journal

Even though talking helps, sometimes we can't find the right person to talk to, who will understand us. In a situation like this, you can always start journaling; it is an emotional release, where you write about your feelings, where you pour your heart out. You will feel more comfortable because no one will judge you; as you start writing, your hands would automatically write something that would surprise you, but those surprising things will help you figure yourself out.

3. Write Again and Again

When journaling, act as if you are telling all these things to a stranger and don't stop just then, write again and again as if you are talking to a different stranger every time you write about your breakup, it will help you gain a different perspective, you would realize many things, but above all, you would learn that whatever happened, happened for a better tomorrow.

4. Let It All Out

When going through a breakup, we all want to scream, shout and let all the anger out, but of course, you can't do all these things in public. So take some time out for yourself, go somewhere private, and talk all the anger, frustration, and tears out. It is normal to feel this way after a breakup, but remember that bottling up your emotions is never good. On the other hand, letting it all out helps you a lot; this would reduce the pressure of all your feelings.

5. Stick To Your Routine

When going through a hard time, we stop following our daily routine, sure it is okay to take some time off from work, but it is not okay to stop eating. When going through a heartbreak, many people stop eating correctly, start sleeping more in the mornings, and just kind of mess their routine. But now is the time to work on yourself, don't stop eating healthy, don't mess up your sleeping habits, and above all, start going to the gym; you can let all the anger and frustration out through some exercise.

6. It Is Time To Make Yourself Feel Special

After a breakup, your sense of self-worth is reduced, a lot of insecurities attack you, but this is not the time to hate yourself; it is the time to love yourself. Don't just sit at home, watching a movie and crying about your breakup; what you can do is get a change. You can go shopping, buy new clothes, jewelry, etc. Get a new haircut, and love the new you. Focus on yourself, become selfish for a while. Now you don't have to think about anyone else, set new goals, and above all, take care of yourself.

Conclusion

Breakups have become very common, so familiar that people sometimes forget what it feels like, but don't worry, and you were not born with this person, try to work on yourself and give yourself the love you deserve. Remember that you are worth someone who cares about you and loves you the way you want to be loved. It is okay to be single; it is the time to try new things and redefine yourself.

Chapter 2:

What to Do When You Are At Different Life Stages In A Relationship

If you've started dating someone a lot older or younger than you and you haven't experienced any bumps along the way, it might be because your relationship is still relatively new.

"The issues begin, I think, to manifest themselves when people start to get into real-life situations. For example, if you don't want kids right away and you're dating someone who never wants them, it might not seem like an issue at the beginning. Still, later on, when you start to feel more ready to start a family, understandably, that tiny little thing can become a really big thing.

Not only that, but some people have had issues dating each other because they were at different stages in their lives. For example, while one might want to go out and dance with friends, the other might have no interest in spending time that way.

There are still ways to make a relationship work if you're at different stages in your life.

That doesn't necessarily mean that the relationship can't work just because you have different interests. For example, a woman said that her husband is ten years younger than her, and they don't have the same taste in music. But they each have friends to talk about those kinds of things, and it works for them.

"If you're dating someone with a big age difference, remember the reasons why you are drawn to that person," "Maybe you are very mature, and individuals your age aren't able to connect with you on a deeper level. Maybe you have a fun, energetic side, and you haven't been able to find a partner your age with similar interests and activities."

We advise that you do some reflection about what you want in the relationship to be clear on that and remind yourself of it when necessary.

Make sure your values, morals, and life goals match up.

"If you want the relationship to be long-term, then make sure that your values, morals, and life goals match.

Ask yourself a few specific questions before diving into something. Things like future goals, where you want to live, if you want a family, if you want religion to be part of your life, and if you see this person fitting in with your family and friends.

It's also important to consider what your relationship will look like down the line. "Big age differences aren't as noticeable when you're both middle-aged, but what happens once one of you is a senior, and the other isn't?" "These are the big picture questions that need to be thought about before you decide to spend your life together."

If you agree with each other on the big things, smaller things like having different tastes in music likely won't be as big of a deal. Just like in any relationship, you don't have to (and won't) agree on everything all the time. Although it might seem like you're farther apart on some topics than you would be if you're closer in age, other factors besides age might play a role in that.

Be prepared for others to comment on your relation.

There's a good chance that people will have opinions about your relationship." They'll ask questions, and they'll make comments that are probably pretty annoying, so be prepared with a response. Depending on who the person is, you might actually feel like you can get into an explanation of the relationship, but other times, it might not feel necessary, so just to be prepared with that,"

Ensure that the relationship's dynamic is equal and that one partner doesn't hold power over the other.

Each partner needs to avoid mothering the other, regardless of who's older or younger in the relationship. It can be difficult for those who take on that role, even among friends, to not act that way with their significant other, but she said that it's important to try to refrain. Sometimes mothering can turn into holding power over your partner, which isn't healthy behavior.

Chapter 3:

Stop Setting Unrealistic Expectations of Your Partner

Are you wondering how to stop unmet expectations from ruining your relationship? Do you find yourself constantly disappointed with your partner and thinking about ending it?

There are ways to stop unmet expectations from ruining your relationship. Here are a few.

1. Identify Your Own

One way to stop unmet expectations from ruining your relationship is by questioning your own. What do you think you need from your partner? Do you need him to give up his friends and hobbies for you? Do you expect to have sex every night? Do you want her to keep the house spotlessly clean as your mother did? Do you expect him to anticipate your every need?

Expectations like these are exactly the things that can kill a relationship. I would encourage you to think about what you want from your partner so that it's clear in your mind. I also want you to consider if your expectations are reasonable.

If your expectations aren't reasonable, your relationship might be dead upon arrival. If you don't know your expectations, your partner will have a hard time reaching them because you might always be moving the goal post. So, before unmet expectations destroy your relationship, make sure you know what yours are.

2. Set Boundaries

I always encourage new couples to set boundaries in their relationships as soon as possible To understand healthy relationship boundaries, look at the four walls of your house. Those walls are the structure that holds your life together. They hold your food and your bed and your possessions, and it's where you live your life.

Healthy boundaries are the same as those four walls of your house. They are the things that support your relationship as it matures. To have a healthy relationship that can grow and be fruitful, it must have structures and boundaries that support it. Healthy boundaries come in many shapes, sizes, and colors.

A few examples:

- Make sure you stay yourself

- Allow yourselves time apart

- Communication is important

- Mutual respect at all times

- Keep the power dynamic equal

- Making time for both sides of the family

- Respecting others friends and hobbies

Of course, each couple needs to decide what works for them, but every couple must establish some boundaries early and stick to them for the sake of their relationship.

3. Be Truthful

You must discuss this with your partner if your expectations aren't being met. One of the most common complaints that I hear from women is 'he should know what I need. I shouldn't have to tell him.' And this, I am afraid, is mostly impossible. Men would love to anticipate and meet our needs, but many of them just don't always have it in them. This is not some deficiency of character but because men have no idea how women think and why. It's a mystery to them, so expecting them to be able to do so will set you up for disaster.

Chapter 4:

Make Time for Your Partner

When I first got into my relationship, I thought my boyfriend and my 100-hour workweek would have to battle it out until the bitter end. Yet somehow, I've managed to maintain both. It turns out there are a lot of weird ways to make time for your partner when you're busy AF. You may have to get creative and resort to some weird measures, but I am living proof that there is no such thing as being too busy for your loved ones.

We all have to run errands. That time is gone from your workday anyway. So, why not use it to show your partner you care instead of just getting what you need? Picking up each other's shampoo and favorite cereal (or, perhaps more practically, take turns picking up groceries and toiletries for the both of you) is one way to connect without needing to make any more time in your schedule.

You spend the same amount of time cooking for two people as you do for one, but since you're feeding two, you *save* time by doing this. Think about it: Instead of cooking every night, you only have to do it every *other* night. Even if you both eat it in front of your computers, making food for each other is a loving gesture that'll make you appreciate each other.

If you live together, you'll probably be sleeping in the same bed anyway. But even if you don't, your dates can consist solely of sleeping if that's what it takes to make time for each other. Or, if you can't sleep through the night with someone else next to you, you can try just sharing nap time.

Even if you don't get around to working out that much, the time you can devote to exercise will help clear your mind, so it's worthwhile if you can make it out for a short run or yoga class. Plus, working out together can boost your attraction by releasing endorphins.

I can't always handle this, especially when I need to feel like nobody wants my attention to focus. But for less intensive tasks, it can be comforting to cuddle up to your significant other while you're working. You can even be each other's sounding boards if you need help coming up with ideas.

This one will not work for everyone. But if you have an office in a similar place, your walk or ride to work can be your bonding time, even if it's just part of the way. Even just a shared walk to the train station can pay off if you think ahead enough to coordinate your trips to and from work.

Chapter 5:

How To Be Your Own Best friend

Why would you want to become your own best friend? There are several benefits to creating your internal support system rather than relying on your partner, friends, or family to be there for you when you're suffering. Having other people's expectations can lead to disappointment, heartbreak, and relationship breakdown if your expectations aren't met.

We all have it in us to give ourselves what we need without seeking it externally.

Of course, it's great if you have a strong support network, but you could still benefit from becoming more self-reliant. And what about if you have no one to turn to for help, or if your current support people are unable to be there for you?

Isn't it far better to know how to support yourself in times of need? Here's how to become your own best friend.

1. Be Nice To Yourself

The first step to becoming a friend is to treat yourself like you would treat a friend. That means that you need to stop being self-critical and beating yourself up. Start by acknowledging your good qualities, talents, and abilities and begin to appreciate your unique self.

When you catch yourself thinking up some nasty self-talk, stop and ask, "Would I say this to my best friend?" If not, then reframe your self-talk to be more supportive and caring.

2. Imagine How You Would Support A Friend In The Same Situation

Think about a loved one, a friend, a family member, someone dear to you and imagine that they are in the same situation you are currently facing. Think about how they're struggling, suffering, and feeling stuck with this problem, then consider how to best offer assistance and advice to them.

Craft the words that you would say to your greatest friend and then say them gently to yourself. Allow yourself to feel supported, and give yourself what you need.

3. Honor Your Needs

Following the theme of considering how you would help a dear friend, **you need to start taking your advice and putting your own needs first**. Do you need a day off from work? A long hot bath? An early night? A wild night? Some time to catch up on your reading, cleaning, gardening, creative projects, social life, or self-care?

Whatever you need, allow yourself to **put it at the top of the list rather than the bottom**. Be there for yourself and make it happen.

4. Send Compassion To The Part of You That is Hurting

Being a friend to yourself involves adopting and mastering the art of self-compassion. Compassion isn't forceful or solution-focused. **Compassion is accepting, peaceful, and loving, without the need to control or change anything**.

Imagine a mother holding a child who has bumped his head. Her compassion is a strong force. She simply holds her child with loving, comforting, gentle arms and whispers, "It will be alright, my love." The child trusts his mother's words just as you learn to trust your own words when speaking to yourself.

Imagine yourself as both the child and the mother simultaneously. Offer compassion at the same time as you open up to receive it.

Use these techniques to become your own best friend and start *being there* **for yourself!**

Chapter 6:

8 Ways To Make The Sex Good

Has your sex life gone stale? Between kids, work, financial pressures, and all the other stressful things, steamy sex may seem like nothing but a fantasy.

Sex isn't just fun, but it's healthy for you too. Every orgasm releases a burst of oxytocin, which instantly improves your mood. Regular rolls in the hay could also improve your heart health, improve your self-esteem, reduce stress and depression, and help you sleep better. As little as only snuggling together underneath the sheets also make you feel closer to your partner and can enhance your sense of intimacy.

If you're stuck in a sexual rut, trust me, you're not alone. While dry spells are expected in any relationship, it's still no consolation for couples experiencing one. The more we get used to someone, the less exciting sex becomes, as familiarity is the death of sex drive. Treating sexual problems is easier now than ever before.

Here are some quick tips to help you reignite the passion your sex life is lacking.

1. Stop Feeling Insecure About Your Body

It really doesn't matter if you haven't lost the baby weight, your specific body parts aren't as high as they used to be, or you have a pimple the size of an egg; it doesn't matter at all. When you're in bed and making love, your partners are not worried about any of your imperfections. To him, you're still the sexiest lady he fell in love with. Besides, it would be best if you understood that his body isn't perfect either. He might have a large belly or a body full of hair. But he doesn't let it get in the way of a good time, and you shouldn't either.

2. Mark A Date

Scheduling sex might sound controlling and not at all fun, but sometimes planning is in order. You book time in your calendar for many things, so why not do the same to prioritize sex? You have to make some room for it and push it forward. Reconnecting with your partner will remind you why you got attracted to him in the first place. Once you have made that sex appointment, the anticipation can be almost as titillating as the event. So, trade some racy texts or leave a sultry voicemail on his cell.

3. Use Lubrication

Often, the vaginal dryness can lead to painful sex, which can, in turn, lead to flagging libido and growing relationship tensions. To avoid any pain during sex or hurting yourself resulting from it, use lubricating liquids and gels. This will make the sex painless and turn on both of you more and more.

4. Practice Touching

Sex therapists use sensate focus techniques that can help you re-establish physical intimacy without feeling pressured. Many of the self-help books and educational videos offer many variations on such exercises. You can also ask your partner to touch you in a manner that you would like to be touched by them, or ask them how they want to be touched. This will give you an idea of the range of pressure from gentle to firm that you should use.

5. Try Different Positions

Sometimes, couples get bored by trying the same 2-3 positions over and over again. Searching and trying new positions will definitely spice up your love life. Developing a repertoire of different sexual positions can enhance your experience of lovemaking and add interest and help you overcome problems. For example, when a man enters his partner from behind, the increased stimulation to the G-spot can help a woman reach orgasm faster.

6. Write Down Your Fantasies

This exercise can help you explore endless possibilities that you think might turn on you and your partner. It could be anything, from reading an erotic book to watching an aroused scene from a movie or TV show that turned you on, you could re-enact them with your partner. Similarly, you could ask your partner about their fantasies and help them fulfill them. This activity is also helpful for people with low desires.

7. Do Kegel Exercises

Both men and women should improve their sexual fitness by exercising their pelvic floor muscles. To do these exercises, tighten the muscle you would use while trying to stop urine in midstream. Hold the contraction for two or three seconds, then release. Repeat 10 times of five sets a day. These exercises can be done anywhere while driving, sitting at your desk, or standing in a check-out line. At home, women may use vaginal weights to add muscle resistance.

8. Try To Relax

Do something soothing and relaxing together before having sex instead of jumping right into it (not that you can't do that), such as playing a game, watching a movie, or having a nice candlelight dinner.

Conclusion

Lack of communication is often what leads to sex droughts in a relationship. Even if you are sexually mismatched, you can get creative and fix those inequities. Stress and busyness of life, among other factors, can also affect sexual intimacy, but there are fruitful ways to overcome setbacks. Don't let fear or embarrassment stop you from trying new stuff. Tap into something simple to get back on track.

Chapter 7:

8 Signs You Need to Call it Quits

Intro:

Most of the times, we stretch our relationship to the point that it becomes unbearable for us to be with someone. We either fear uncertainty or be lonely that we push our boundaries of tolerance; the sole reason for doing that is to avoid pain. You need to take care of your happiness. The whole point of being with someone is to be happy. If there is no passion or romance left and your relationship feels stagnant, it is time for you to call it quits because from that point on, your relationship is only going to degrade, and you should leave before things take a turn for the worse. If you feel that you deserve better and have unmet emotional needs, there is no reason to continue the relationship. Even if you try your hardest, you can not twist the reality. If you are having trouble figuring out whether you should call it quits or not, we are going to give you 7 reasons why you should call it quits!

1. Lost Trust:

One of the essential parts of a relationship is "trust" it works like glue and holds a relationship together. Trust assures you that a person is loyal to you, and no matter what happens, they will always stay by your side. The long-term survival of a relationship is not possible without trust. If you do not trust your partner, you will doubt their actions, and it will be bad for you and them because you will be acting like a detective checking upon them all the time, they will lose their freedom, and you will lose your peace of mind. If you do not trust your partner, you should just let them go.

2. You feel Unhappy:

All relationships feel amazing in the beginning. Later, you get to see their partner for who they are. The point of getting into a relationship is to feel happy and complete. If you feel anxious and full of pain, then what is the point of this relationship? You will start feeling lonely even when your partner is with you. If you feel sad and disappointed most of the time rather than happy and sad, it just means your partner does not think about you anymore. If you need to leave your partner to find peace, then it's time to call it quits.

3. Lack of Support:

It is essential to have a supportive and understanding partner if you want your relationship to grow. Your relationship becomes ten times harder if your partner does not believe in your dreams most of your time and energy will be consumed in convincing them that you are capable of doing that. If someone important in your life will continuously discourage you, negativity and self-doubt will surround you. Being with the wrong person will make you feel worthless all the time. If someone is hindering your growth and pulling you down, then you should cut them loose.

4. Zero Communication:

Lack of communication will lead to a lot of misunderstandings. If you do not sit with your partner to speak your mind with them, your emotions are bottled up and even when you do, they do not try to understand your perspective and instead play blame games this just results in hurting you more. If there is increased misunderstanding and you have tried to solve the issue multiple times, and the result is always the same, there is a high chance things are not going to change in the near future. There is a difference between not trying to communicate and not trying to understand the other person. If the case is later, then it's time to leave them for good.

5. Controlling Behavior:

It might be a bit difficult for you to identify between a caring partner and a controlling partner. But we are here to make things easy for you. A controlling partner always interferes in your business and will criticize you even for little things. The worst thing they will do is isolate you from your family and friends, and sometimes they will even try to turn them against you. They are insecure, so they will also ask you to not talk to certain people, mostly of the opposite gender. Plus, you will have to explain yourself a lot, and if you do not, it will lead to a fight.

6. Zero Efforts:

The key factor that leads to the growth of a relationship is an active effort from both sides. It is all in the efforts you make to get to know them, keep each other happy and take an interest in each other's life. A relationship does not survive if there is not enough effort from both sides. If there is a one-sided effort, then there will be a lot of burden on the person trying to make it work, and as a result, this will drain your energy and exhaust yourself. If your partner does not go beyond their comfort zone to be there for you will suffocate you.

7. Different Life Paths:

If you and your partner are on the same page, the relationship will go a long way. At first, you do not really care about the future because you are so engrossed in your relationship, but when you realize that this might affect your goals, it is difficult to carry on. You will think about it every day, and it will consume you, but you should remember no relationship is greater than your happiness.

Conclusion:

All of the relationships and people are different from each other some choose to leave a relationship for their dreams, and some might give up their dreams for love. What you need to do is find out what makes you happy and works for you. You need to set limits for yourself, and beyond those limits, you will not compromise or bend yourself. You should never forget the entire point of being in a relationship is to be happy, and so you can finally have someone who understands you. These are the two things you should never compromise on.

Chapter 8:

7 Tips To Get Over Your Ex

When you get together with someone, it feels like that relationship will never come to an end, but sometimes things just do not work out the way we wanted them to. Break-ups and ending all contact is probably one of the hardest things to do. Sometimes, you start obsessing over them, over the life they might be leading without you. But one thing a person should remember after a bad break-up is that you weren't born with that person; you have lived without them and can do the same again; it just needs a bit of work and time. Here are several ways to get over your ex.

1. Social Media Detox

The most common way of communication is now social media, but we all know its disadvantages. It has made it hard for people to move on; seeing your ex again and again in pictures on social media may provoke some unwanted feelings. So the best way to not feel that way is to get off of social media for a while or unfollow your ex; commit yourself not to check their page or the page where there is a chance you might see them. You just need to gather some willpower and try not to stalk them, which will quickly help you move on.

2. Let Go Of The Memories

When you first start dating someone, it feels right and like you are living in a fantasy. The beginning of a relationship brings many expectations along with it; there are things you expect from your partner and something that your partner expects from you. But when these expectations are crushed, one may feel hurt. A person starts to miss someone when they remember the great times together, so you need to remember that you broke up for a reason. Try to remember what your ex did or didn't do that lead to this break-up. There is always a reason behind a break-up, so place the causes, and you will find yourself realizing that it ended for a good reason.

3. Get Rid Of The Things That Remind You Of Your Ex

In a relationship, we all receive gifts and heartwarming cards and letters, which may make you feel happy at that time, but after a break-up, these cards and gifts may serve as a reminder of your ex and bring back some unwanted but sweet memories. These precious memories can lead you to believe that you miss them. So as soon as you break up with someone, get rid of their reminders. This can include small gifts, cards, clothing because these can lead to obsession.

4. Love Yourself

Loving yourself sounds like a total cliché, but you can never move on from someone without loving yourself. When someone dumps you, you might feel lowly about yourself, and the self-worth you had in mind may get dropped. As much as it sounds easy, it is not. True happiness and love need to come from within. You need to start appreciating yourself, connect with yourself again, and you will start feeling that you don't want anybody else's love to survive because your own is enough.

5. Visualise Your Future Without Them

In a relationship, people make plans and set goals together. So when you break up, you might feel confused as to what to do next, as all your dreams of the future include them. When trying to move on, remember you had a life before them, a life with goals to be achieved. Visualize your future without them; try to set some goals for yourself. Think about all the things you can do now that you couldn't have done with your ex. Visualizing your future without them will help you accept that this relationship is over. You may have a lot of options now that you no longer feel tied to someone. You can set your priorities again.

6. Don't Contact Your Ex

You can set a few rules for yourself when you break up with someone, and these rules should include a no-contact rule at least until you've moved on. Do not contact your ex until you have moved on and accepted everything. Hearing their voice can bring back a lot of memories that will not let you move on.

7. Move Or Redecorate

If you used to share your living space with your ex, literally everything in your house will remind you of them. Move out if you can, but if moving out is not an option, you can redecorate the home, change the furniture positions, and buy some new accessories for the house. Redecorating the house is an activity that you may feel excited about, buy the things you have always wanted but couldn't because of your ex.

Conclusion

Bad break-ups can mess someone up but fortunately, working on yourself can help you move on, so remember that you are a complete person without them, and you don't need them to live your life.

Chapter 9:

6 Signs You Are Ready To Move To The Next Step In A Relationship

If you're dating someone long enough, chances are you might know them well now and are ready to take your relationship to the next level. You both work out well together through all the ups and downs, connect with each other, and make each other's life wonderful. So whether you're thinking about making your relationship official by introducing them to your family and friends, moving in with them, or even getting engaged, it can both be scary and exciting when you think about making the relationship serious and taking that leap of faith.

If you feel that you have a healthy relationship, you can't imagine your life without your partner and are in a good place emotionally, then say no more. Here are some signs to convince you that you should up your game!

1. You Both Trust Each Other Fully

Being able to trust someone entirely isn't as easy as it sounds, especially in times like these and the world we're living in right now. The most significant quality one can look for in a partner is how much they value our trust. If you are confident that your partner will always have your back and you can be weak and vulnerable in front of them, maybe you should consider taking the next step. If you have told something to them in confidence and they don't share the information with anyone, and likewise if you do the same, then you both are fortunate.

2. You Support Each Other Through The Good and Bad

Having someone by your side who you know would always support you, no matter what is nothing short of a blessing. Your partner has always comforted and consoled you through the negative phases and cherished and cheered you through the positive ones. Even if they were dealing with their problems, they made sure you were okay first. Most of the time, we tend to emotionally drain out or become frustrated by being there for people. But with your partner, you are always ready to lend a helping hand and even an ear, listen to all of their problems and shortcomings and support them every step of the way.

3. You Both Apologize To Each Other When Needed

One of the major signs of a toxic relationship is when your partner doesn't apologize or take accountability, even if they know they are wrong. These relationships tend to have a dead end. You might have noticed that your partner admits when wrong and apologizes, even if not straight away; they do it sooner or later. They try to sort out the arguments and fights calmly and try to listen to your point of views and opinions too, instead of forcing theirs on you. They make sure that you're okay after the fight and may even make small gestures to make you feel that they are guilty and you are more important than any of the arguments you both get into.

4. You Give Each Other Space

You both have a level of freedom and independence both within and outside the relationship. You both aren't on each other's throat and nerves every second. You both have different hobbies and passions that you pursue. You both can meet your friends alone or hang out by yourself, without stressing over if your partner would mind. This is a sign of a healthy relationship when you don't keep buzzing your partner with unlimited calls or texts, ask them about their whereabouts, or cling to them all day.

5. You're On The Same Page With Them

Even if you and your partner don't share the same goals, hobbies, dreams, passions, or even the same views and opinions, you're still on the same page with them about your values and future. For example, both of you have discussed either having children or no children in the future, getting a destination wedding or a simple one, moving out of the city or across the country, or settling in the same spot where you both are right now. Agreeing on the same stuff shows that you both prioritize the same things and are compatible with stepping up your relationship.

6. You Feel Safe With

One of the signs that your relationship is ready for the next step is the feeling of comfort and security when you are with them. You can be your utter authentic self with them without fearing that they might judge you or dislike you. You have shown all of your sides to them, the good and the bad, and they still love you regardless. They like your quirks and don't get annoyed or irritated by your behavior. You also have accepted your partner's flaws and imperfections and still look at them the same way.

Conclusion

Taking the next big step in a relationship could be confusing and stressful, especially when you find yourself confused and unclear. So if you have found someone worthy of your time and energy, don't let them go. Instead, cling onto them, and make efforts to keep your relationship floating.

PART 3

Chapter 1:

6 Ways To Flirt With Someone

No matter how confident and bold we assume ourselves to be, we tend to freeze up and utter a wimpy 'hey' when we see our crush approaching us. Flirting doesn't always come easily to everyone, and there's always struggle, awkwardness, and shyness that follows. But, some people are natural-born flirters and just get the dating thing right.

Knowing how to flirt and actually showing someone that you're interested in them sexually or romantically can be a minefield. But once you get your hands on it, you'll probably become an expert in no time. If you struggle with flirting, we've got some tips to help you master the art of flirting and getting your crush's attention. Below are some ways to flirt with someone successfully.

Be Confident But Mysterious

There's nothing sexier than someone who has a lot of confidence. Of course, I'm not talking about being too overconfident, and it will tend to push people away from you. But if you're strutting down the halls as you own them, your crush (and everyone else) will notice you. Don't give away too much of yourself while being confident. People tend to get intrigued by someone who gives off mysterious vibes. They show their interest in you and avail every opportunity to try to get to know you better. This will lead to you having a chance to make up a good conversation with your crush and even flirt with them in between.

Show That You're Interested In Their Life

Who doesn't love compliments and talking about themselves all the time? We come along with people who mostly like to talk than to listen. If you get a chance to talk to your crush, don't waste it. Ask them questions about their life, get to know their views and ideas about certain things like politics, fashion, controversies, show that you're genuinely interested in them. They will love your curious nature and would definitely look forward to having another conversation with you. This will also give your brownie points of getting to know them better.

Greet Them Whenever You Pass Them

Seeing your crush approach you or simply seeing them standing in the halls can be the scariest feeling ever. You will probably follow your gut reaction and become nervous; either you'll walk past them hurriedly or look down at your phone and pretend like you're in the middle of a text conversation battle. But you have to ignore those instincts, and you have to look up at them and simply smile. You don't have to indulge yourself in an extensive conversation with them. Just taking a second to wave or say hi can be more than enough to get yourself on your crush's radar, as you will come off as polite to them.

Make Ever-So-Slight Contact

The sexiest touches are often those electric ones that come unexpectedly, not the intentional ones that might make someone uncomfortable. Unnecessary touches can be a turn-on because they signal a willingness to venture beyond the safe boundaries that we usually maintain between ourselves and others. But be careful not to barge into them accidentally. Small, barely-there touches that only the two of you notice are the best. Let your foot slightly touch theirs or lightly brush past them.

Compliment Them

While everyone loves receiving compliments, try not to go overboard, or they would be more likely to squirm in their seat rather than ask you out. You should compliment them lightly about their outfit or fragrance or their features or personality, but keep the subtle flirtation for when the time and moment is right. Giving them compliments would make them think that you're interested in them and want to step up the equation with them.

Look At Them

Experts suggest that we look and then look away three times to get someone's attention. According to the Social Issues Research Centre, maintaining too much eye contact while flirting is people's most common mistake. Our eyes make a zigzag motion when we meet someone new - we look at them from eye to eye and then the nose. With friends, we look below their eye level to include the nose and mouth. The subtle flirt then widens that triangle to incorporate parts of the body. Please don't stare at someone too intensely, or else you'll end up making them feel uncomfortable.

Conclusion

It might seem nerve-wracking to put yourself out there and start flirting, but fear not! It's normal to get nervous around someone whom you like. Follow the above ways to seem confident and pull off a successful flirtation. Know the importance of keeping a balance between revealing your feelings and keeping the person you like intrigued.

Chapter 2:

7 Reasons Why Men Cheat

Men and women may cheat for different reasons, but it's likely due to the way men and women are socialized rather than any innate differences between them. The more we, as a society, move away from socialization and patriarchy, the less we see those gender differences in cheating behavior. However, nonetheless, research shows that men are more likely to cheat than women. The ratio is 20% of men have admitted to cheating compared to 13% of women.

We should never forget that our minds are more resilient than we give them credit for. Cheating in a relationship is solely that person's fault, no matter the circumstances. It can always be avoided if the person wants to. There are many reasons why men cheat, along with what defines cheating and signs to watch out for. Here are some reasons and behaviors that might apply to people of all genders but could be relevant to men.

1. They're Looking For A Way Out

Sometimes the first step for a man to get out of a relationship is to cheat. Although people of all genders might cheat, for this reason, men are most likely to do it. This is because men are less likely to have difficult conversations with their partners and seldom tell their own needs in a relationship. So, they see cheating as the only way out. Instead of having to bear the difficult conversation with their partner when they're done with their relationship, they escape through it all by the act of cheating and having an affair.

2. They're Looking For A Connection

Cheating doesn't always happen for physical reasons only, despite what gender norms might tell us about men. Feeling unseen, unheard, or disconnected from their partners can also contribute as a factor for it. Men are much less likely to have a sound social support system, and those things can hurt and make them go into a zone where they feel protected. In those instances, if a woman shows compassion and support, they welcome her with open arms. It might start with a friendship with someone who will make him feel better about himself, and hence, an emotional connection forms.

3. They Have Sociopathic or Narcissistic Traits

If a partner has cheated, there could be more than just finding a way out of their relationship. There can be narcissistic tendencies or sociopathic traits involved. They could be someone who doesn't care about their partner's feelings, and they might do it simply because they want to. When an opportunity to cheat presents itself, they go towards it without giving a damn about their partner.

4. Revenge Cheating

Some people act on their impulses and cheat out of anger, jealousy, or desire revenge. It's not necessary that their partner might have cheated on them; even if they have done something slight to upset them (like having a close friendship with another man), they'll end up cheating on their partner to make a point.

5. Struggles With Substance Abuse

Cheating becomes more likely if one is dealing with a substance abuse problem. Substance addiction can create an impulse-driven and more immature version of ourselves. Many relationships tend to fall apart if one of the two partners has become addicted to a substance and acts subconsciously on their impulse.

6. They Seek Validation

If someone is not getting validation in their relationship, then insecurity and low self-esteem can drive them to cheat. If they don't feel attracted enough to their partner, they may cheat to seek external validation. Sexual issues can also cause someone to look for someone newer to prove themselves to.

7. They're Emotionally Immature

Emotional immaturity is sometimes the core of why men cheat. Since childhood, men are expected and taught not to talk about their feelings and emotions. This inability to speak leads to several issues and conflicts in their relationships. By the time you know it, they are having an affair and cheating on their significant other. Cheating can be an essential consequence of poor judgment, lack of willpower, self-control, and immaturity. A mature man will always talk about his feelings and resolve conflicts and issues with his partner.

Conclusion:

Being cheated on can be the worst trauma anyone can experience, and there can be so many reasons it might have happened in different relationships and contexts. But no matter the reason, it cannot be denied that infidelity forces both of you to step back. Analyze what went wrong and decide how you both want to move forward from there.

Chapter 3:

6 Ways To Deal With Rude People

Rudeness is not a quality everybody likes; on the contrary, most people tend to stay away from rude people, so they don't have to deal with them, but sometimes, we haven't got any options, avoiding them isn't an option. You can meet rude people in your work offices, schools, colleges, or any public place. You have to deal with them. When someone is disrespectful to us, all we want to do is snap back at them, but that would make you just like them. Here are a few ways to deal with rude people.

1. Try To Be Understanding

We have got those bad days when we don't want to talk to anyone and when someone talks to us, we respond a bit rudely even if we don't realize it. The person who's being rude to you could also be going through something right now. The best you can do is be understanding and give them some space. Eventually, they would realize and would apologize. If they don't apologize and continue being rude, just let it go; you can't change how someone wants to talk to people. Everybody has their habits. Even though being rude is not that good practice, it is still a habit, and to change a pattern, a person needs time and willpower.

2. Call Them Out On Their Behavior

As mentioned before, sometimes we don't realize when we ate being rude to someone, but that doesn't make us wrong. It is just that we are going through a particular phase in our life that causes us to be that way. So if someone is rude to you, call them out on their rudeness; if they care, they will indeed apologize. If they don't want to be sorry, then don't get upset, limit your contact with them, like talking to them only when necessary because it's difficult to completely stay away from that rude person if he is a co-worker or a neighbor.

3. Don't Backbite

Don't talk bad about that person behind his back to someone else. Firstly it would spread rumors, and people would not hesitate to gossip. Secondly, talking behind someone's back is also considered rude, so if you talk behind that person's back, what is the difference between you and that rude person. Thirdly, when you talk bad about someone, it will only cause the situation to get worse than it already is.

4. Avoid The Rude Person

Even when you call them out on your behavior but the person is still impolite towards you, don't stress; walk away. If they are rude, then it is their problem, not yours. You don't have you worry about it because there is nothing you can do. Just walk away and don't give that person the slightest chance to talk to you. Indeed, when everyone starts walking away from him, he would realize that this habit is not causing any good and would make an effort to change and become better.

5. Be More Kind

This way is more than complex, of course; who would want to be nice to someone who isn't nice to you, but when you offer some extra kindness, you will set an example for that person. Everybody loves a kind person. After a while of your service, the person would realize that you are kind and don't deserve his rudeness. The other person would eventually calm down and surely will follow your lead. It's hard to be rude to someone who is too kind towards you.

6. Rudeness Is Nothing New

Since the beginning of time, rudeness has been a part of human nature; there is nothing new. No matter what you do, you will always find rude people everywhere you go. All you need to do is accept that this is nothing new and you can't change the way these people think, maybe it is their habit, and perhaps they will change this with time, but there is nothing you can do about it, so don't fret.

Conclusion

Don't take the words of rude people to heart. The world is full of rudeness; no matter what you do, you can't get rid of them. But there is one thing you can do, be the kind and loving person that you are. Don't be rude to them, just be kind towards them. Indeed with time, everybody realizes their bad habits. And don't worry about it, at least you are not among the rude people.

Chapter 4:

6 Ways To Deal With Betrayal

Betrayal is a strong word. And the most challenging part of it is recovery. Healing from something someone has done to you that you were not in favor of can be as hard as counting the number of hair on your head. The first thing that comes in our way is our emotions. Anger, rage, and regret. But, what can one do to save themselves from such a move? They can only be careful with the people around them. Trust issues have always been challenging to deal with. And betrayal only fuels that fire. We often turn to others for support, and sometimes they turn out to be deceivers. It may leave us unprotected.

No doubt that betrayal changes someone to some extinct. The person may feel insecurities within themselves. They start to doubt and stress themselves. It often leads to self-harm, too, at times. And the most severe of them all would be anxiety. Because no matter what, we can't ignore the fact that someone has lied to us and made us believe them. Betrayal is painful. And it's common to have experienced it once in your life. When someone you trusted with your secrets or emotions has broken that trust, that feeling of not being valued enough makes us hate that person, whether they did it intentionally or unintentionally. But there can be some ways to deal with betrayal.

1. Take Time For Emotional Improvement

After a heartbreak, what we need is time. Time to think, time to process, and time to heal. We can't instantly forget about anything that has happened to us. "Time heals all wounds." And that is precisely what we should do. Take a break. Try to do things you want. Make yourself feel light and collected. Stay away from the person who hurt you. This way, it will help you bury that memory quickly. Try to think about it as little as possible. Make sure you have other things on your mind instead. Rearrange your priorities from the start. This time you believe in yourself more than you felt in that person.

2. Overcome Self-Hatred

It is often that you would feel hatred towards yourself. Because you sometimes believe that it was your fault, to begin with. The thing with betrayal is that it is one-sided. The other person can do nothing but suffer. Naturally, you would be pitying yourself for their actions and feeling insecure. But it's not worth your time or emotion. You need to get a hold of yourself and talk some sense into yourself.

3. Try To Forgive and Forget

We all know that it is not as easy as it sounds, but it is more beneficial. When someone betrays us, we feel the need to take revenge. Hurt them the way they hurt us. But nothing can be as comforting as forgetting it ever happened. We all will remember a part of it, but it doesn't have to come between your life. It takes a lot of determination to forgive someone you don't want to ignore, but you will see the pros of it in the future. If you decide you take revenge, then it will leave you guilty and regretful in the future.

4. Ask For Help From The Trusted

It may be difficult for you to trust anyone after being betrayed. But you can always go to someone for comfort. If a possible third party can support you, don't hesitate to reach out to them. Make sure you talk about it with someone so you can take advice and feel light. It will help you to deal with the situation quickly. It will give you the peace of mind that will help you all along the journey ahead. It is recommended to talk with someone who had a betrayal in their life.

5. Acknowledge, Don't React

There is a significant difference between responding and reacting. We should be in control of our emotions. We need to acknowledge our feelings. After betrayal, our senses are more likely to be mixed up, leaving us confused. But that is a recipe for disaster. It will only be harmful to you to react without analyzing the situation appropriately. You can't ignore the fact that you have been hurt, but you will feel calmer by the time.

6. Be Careful Next Time

No one can ensure that we won't get hurt again. But we can be careful around people. That doesn't necessarily mean having trust issues with people but detecting the people who can hurt you. And with each time, you will get better and better at dealing with betrayal. It would help if you felt those emotions to overcome them every single time. And after each series of betrayals, you will become stronger than before.

Conclusion

Betrayal can be heart-wrenching, but it should not stop you from being happy in life. Cry and grieve for a day or two. And then get up again as a stronger person. Believe in yourself. Let go of the past and focus on your future, for it can bring much more happiness.

Chapter 5:

6 Ways To Deal With Arguments In A Relationship

Arguments are common in all kinds of relationships, be it with your parents, siblings, friends, or partner. Some degree of conflict can even be healthy as it shows that both of the partners are expressing themselves, rather than keeping their emotions fester and everything inside. Fighting consistently can also lead to a problematic relationship where you and your partner wouldn't be at peace. And if handled poorly, it can also become the cause of the downfall of your relationship.

It's normal to argue with your loved ones from time to time, but if the arguing is continuing at an unhealthy pace, or your disagreements are ending up in hostile silence, or worse, a screaming match, then it can take a severe toll on your life and affect it. Learning ways to handle disagreements constructively must be crucial in every relationship. Conflict is inevitable; it's how you deal with it that counts. Here are some of the ways to deal with arguments in a relationship.

1. Find Out Why You're Arguing In The First Place

Sometimes we look at the superficial layer of the issue, not the deeper layers that might discover the real reason behind the argument. If you and your partner frequently argue or about the same things, it can be good to evaluate what really is causing the conflict. You should see if the argument is really what you think you're arguing about, or are other factors involved too? Are there other things happening in your relationship that are worrying or frustrating you? You may want to consider other influences too, like, are there any significant changes happening in your life that's putting extra pressure on you? Maybe you're spending less time with your partner, and the cause of your arguments is sometimes unknown. Or perhaps you're both struggling with something that you aren't ready to talk about. Looking at the broader context of your situation and seeing past your emotions can be a great way to get to the bottom of what's going on.

2. Talking It Over

Talking calmly and constructively when you are actually overwhelmed and feeling emotional can be really difficult. It would be best if you gave yourself and your partner some time to cool off before starting the discussion again. It's essential to open up your feelings to your partner and ask them to do the same. If something's bothering you, you can always talk to your partner calmly and understandably rather than keeping it inside and only giving them hints. No one likes a guessing game in a relationship. Being vocal about your issues and hearing about your partner's, and then talking and sorting it out is critical.

3. Try To Start The Discussion Amicably

Don't start bypassing sarcastic or critical comments, mocking them, or aiming them with gun fires. It can only worsen the situation. Your partner may feel like you're insulting them and not respecting their emotions. Don't take the arguments personally and make it all about yourself. Try to be calm and patient and start by saying something positive like, "I feel like we have been arguing a lot lately; maybe we should discuss what's causing us both trouble and get back to our loving selves." This will not only make your partner feel important but also might end the argument all in all.

4. Try To See Things From Your Partner's Perspective

A conversation is likely to end up being productive if both partners aren't ready to listen to each other. It can be tempting to get your point across, but if you're looking to resolve things, you should take the time to hear about your partner's side too. They might have an entirely different perspective, but you need to understand it if you want to get to the root of what's causing you both to fight. Try to validate each other's feelings by hearing each other and comforting each other.

5. Keep Tabs On Physical Feelings

If the argument is getting too heated, take some time out to calm yourself and then continue once you're both feeling better. Don't pass remarks that you might later regret, or it could make your fight worse. It could end up leaving both of you seriously hurt.

6. Be Prepared to Compromise

Giving ground by both partners is often the only way to resolve a conflict. If both of you stick rigidly to your desired outcome, the fight would never come to an end. Sometimes, an imperfect solution can be better than having no solution at all. To move past things, one or both of the partners must compromise a little.

Conclusion

It can take some time and practice to disagree calmly and constructively and to change the negative behaviors. But if you stick with working together better, it can produce positive changes in your relationship. Forgive yourself and your partner and move on.

Chapter 6:

6 Ways To Be More Confident In Bed

Confidence is something a lot of people inherit naturally, while others could work on. When you're confident and comfortable in your skin, people assume that you have a reason to be, and then they react and respect you accordingly. You can be confident all you want at work or on dates, but what about being confident in bed? Being confident sexually can be enjoyable for both you and your partner. It isn't just at ease sexual, but also it's comfortable with the way you express and experience your sexuality.

Sexual confidence can be measured by how authentically you can relate intimately either with yourself or your partner and how pure and vulnerable you are in that sexual space where you feel like giving your 100 percent to be yourself and communicate the pleasure you desire. Building your confidence in bed can crucially improve your sex life. Here are some tips on how to be more confident in bed.

1. Do What You're Already Confident In

Even if you are insecure and think you lack sexual skills, there must be at least a tiny thing that you might be good at. Maybe you don't feel confident enough about your kissing skills, but you're a great cuddler, or perhaps you feel shaky about touching and teasing but are good vocally. Focus on what you're good at and polish that skill every time you're in bed with your partner. This will help you boost your confidence and might even convince you to try something new with them.

2. Try Something New

Once you start considering yourself as the master of that one skill you have been practicing, you would end up craving to try new things. Start with the things you're less comfortable with; maybe stepping out of your comfort zone might be enjoyable for you after all. You neither have to perfect the skill nor be a master of it, just trying it out can be fun in itself. It might be helpful to broaden the sexual script so that it doesn't look the same every time and bore your partner, but instead, trying new things can be an excellent adventure for you as well as your partner.

3. Laugh It Off If You Trip Up

You can't be good at everything you try in bed, nor should you be. What matters is how well you keep your attitude, and if you can have fun with it and have a great laugh if things go south, that's an achievement in itself. If you have already built up consistent self-confidence, then you can laugh it out loud on something that you can't get a grip on. After all, there might always be some things you'll be bad at and others in which you'll be a master.

4. Focus On What You Love About Your Body

There are instances where we will be utterly insecure about our bodies and features. There are some physical traits that we don't like but have made peace with, while others that we want but don't appreciate enough. The next time you look in the mirror, focus more on what you like about your face and body, be confident in them, and the things you don't like about yourself will vanish automatically.

5. Wear What Makes You Feel Confident

There is no particular stuff you have to wear or the way you have to look to feel more confident, but if you wear a look that you think looks great, you must go with it. Chances are, you will start feeling better about yourself instantly. If you feel more confident wearing lipstick, then wear it to bed, or if you think sexier wearing a lotion, use it before bed. Do whatever makes you feel like a total hottie.

6. Repeat A Mantra

We have all heard of the phrase "fake it till you make it." So, there's no harm in faking affirmations till you start believing in them. Keep repeating "I'm confident, I've got this" till it gets through. Affirmations increase how positively we feel about ourselves.

Conclusion

The task of becoming confident may seem daunting, but these small sub-tasks are an easy way to start. Another plus point is once you have practiced these techniques in bed, the confidence will spill over into every area of your life.

Chapter 7:

6 Tips To Find The One

Finding someone who matches our criteria can be a difficult task. We always look for a person who is a knight in shining armor. And by time, we make our type. We are finding someone who looks and behaves like our ideal one. We always fantasize about our right one. No matter how hard it may seem to find someone, we should never lose hope. Sharing is always beneficial. And if you trust someone enough to share your life with them, then it's worth the risk to be taken. The person you chose depends upon you only. The advice can only give you an idea, and you have to act on your own.

Now, when looking for someone from scratch can be difficult for many of us. That person can either be the wrong one or the right one. Only time can tell you that. But you both need to grow together to know if you can survive together. And if not, then separation is the only possible way. But if you find the right one, then it will all be good. You have to have faith in yourself. Be your wingman and go after whatever you desire.

1. Be Patient

When looking for someone you want to spend your time with, someone you want to dedicate a part of your life to, you have to devote your time looking for the one. Be patient with everyone you meet so you will get to know them better. They will be more open towards you when you give them time to open. Doing everything fast will leave you confused. Don't only talk with them. Notice their habits, share secrets and trust them. They will be more comfortable around you when they think that you are willing to cooperate.

2. Keep Your Expectations Neutral

When you find someone for you, they can either leave you disappointed or satisfied. That all depends on your expectations. If you wait for prince charming and get a knight, then you will be nothing but uncomfortable with them. Keep them neutral. Try to make sure that you get to know a person before passing your judgment.

3. Introduce Them To Your Friends

The people who love you tend to get along together. The first thing we do after finding a competitor is telling a friend. We usually go for the people our loved one has chosen for us. While finding the one is all you. They can play a part in giving advice, but they can't decide for you. When we see one, we want everyone to get to know them.

4. Don't Be Discouraged

You are 30 and still haven't found anyone worth your time. If so, then don't get discouraged. That love comes to us when we least expect it. You have to keep looking for that one person who will brighten your days and keep you happy. Please don't go looking for it. It will come to you itself and will make you happy.

5. Look Around You

Sometimes our journey of finding the one can be cut short when we see the one by our side—someone who has been our friend or someone who was with us all along. You will feel happier and more comfortable with finding the right person within your friend. It will make things much more manageable. And one day, you will realize that he was the one all this time. Sometimes we can find one in mutual friends. They may be strangers, but you know a little about them already. However, finding the one within your friend can save you a lot of trouble.

6. Keep The Sparks Fresh

Whatever happens, don't let your spark die because it will become the source of your compassion. It will make a path for you to walk on with your ideal one. Keep that passion, that love alive. If there is no spark, then you will live a life without any light. So, make your partner and yourself feel that compassion in your growth.

Conclusion

Finding one can be a difficult job, but once we find them, they can make us the happiest in the world. And if that person is honest with you, then there is nothing more you should need in one. You can always change your partner until you find the one because they are always their ones too. You have to focus on finding your own.

Chapter 8:

6 Signs Your Love Is One Sided

While some things are better one-sided, like your favorite ice-cream cone that you don't want to share, your high school diary that knows all your enemies and crushes, and a game of solitaire. But a healthy relationship? Now that should be a two-sided situation. Unfortunately, when you're stuck in a one-sided relationship, it becomes easy to fool yourself every day that what you are experiencing is normal, when in reality, it could actually be toxic or even unworthy and loveless.

They could physically be sitting next to you, but you will find yourself being alone because of your emotional needs not being taken care of. Even though you have committed yourself to your partner, there's a fundamental difference between being selfless in love and giving it all without receiving anything at all. It might be possible that you're in denial, but the below signs of your one-sided love are hard to ignore.

1. You're Constantly Second-Guessing Yourself

If you don't get enough reassurance from your partner and constantly wonder if you are pretty enough, or intelligent enough, or funny enough, and always trying to live up to your partner's expectations, then you're definitely in a one-sided relationship. You tend to focus all of your energy and attention on being liked instead of being your true self and nurtured by your partner. It would be best if you always were your authentic self so the people who genuinely deserve you can get attracted to you and get relationships that match the true you.

2. You Apologize More Than Needed

Everyone makes mistakes. We are not some divine creatures who are all perfect and have no flaws. Sometimes you're at fault, sometimes your partner is. But if you end up saying sorry every single time, even if you had no idea about the fight, then maybe take a deeper look at your relationship. You may think that you're saving your relationship by doing this, but trust me, this is a very unhealthy sign. Cori Dixon-Fyle, founder and psychotherapist at Thriving Path, says, "Avoiding conflict results in dismissing your feelings." Solving fights should always be a team approach and not just one person's responsibility.

3. You're Always Making Excuses For Your Partner

Playing defense is excellent, but only on a soccer team. Suppose you are doing it constantly for your partner and justifying their behaviors to your circle of friends, family, and work colleagues. In that case, you're overlooking something that they are most likely seeing. If the people in your life are constantly alarming you, then maybe you should focus on your partner and see where the signs are coming from.

4. You Feel Insecure About Your Relationship

If you are never indeed at ease with your partner and often question the status of your relationship, then it's a clear sign that you are in a one-sided relationship. If you focus more on analyzing yourself, becoming more alluring, and choosing words or outfits that will keep your partner desiring you, then it's a major red flag. To feel unsettled and all-consumed in a relationship is not only exhausting, but it's also sustainable. Feeling constantly depleted in your relationship is also a sign that it's one-sided.

5. You're Giving Too Much

Giving too much and expecting just a little can never work in the long run. Suppose you're the only one in the relationship who makes all the plans. Do all the chores, remember all the important dates and events, consider stopping or making your partner realize that they aren't giving much in the relationship. Often when people give, they have some expectations in the back of their mind that the giving will be returned, but things fall apart when the other person never had those intentions. It's normal for a short while for one partner to carry the load more than the other; all relationships go through such stages, but constantly engaging in it is unhealthy.

6. You're Never Sure About How They Are Feeling

You can't read people's minds, nor are the communications transparent; you may end up overthinking their behaviors towards you and may be confused about how they're truly feeling. This uncertainty would cause you to dismiss your feelings in favor of thinking about them. This connection may be filled with guessing and speculations rather than knowing reality and seeing where they genuinely stand.

Conclusion

The best way to fix a one-sided relationship is to step away and focus on your self-worth and self-growth instead of trying to water a dead plant. You must focus on flourishing your own life instead of shifting your all to your partner. Your mental health should be your priority.

Chapter 9:

6 Signs You Are Emotionally Unavailable

In times of need, all we want is emotional comfort. The people around us mainly provide it. But the question is, will we support them if the need arises? You might be emotionally unavailable for them when they need you. It is necessary to have some emotional stability to form some strong bonds. If you are emotionally unapproachable, you will have fewer friends than someone you stand mentally tall. It is not harmful to be emotionally unavailable, but you need to change that in the long run. And for that, you need to reflect on yourself first.

It would help if you always were your top priority. While knowing why you are emotionally unapproachable, you need to focus on yourself calmly. Giving respect and talking is not enough for someone to rely on you. You need to support them whenever needed. Talk your mind with them. Be honest with them. But not in a rude way, in a comforting way. So, next time they will come to you for emotional support and comfort. If you are relating to all these things, then here are some signs that confirm it.

1. You Keep People At A Distance

It is usual for an emotionally unavailable person to be seen alone at times. They tend to stay aloof at times; that way, they don't have to be emotionally available. And even if you meet people, you always find it challenging to make a bond with them. You might have a few friends and family members close to you. But you always find meeting new people an emotionally draining activity. You also might like to hang out with people, but opening up is not your forte. If you are emotionally unavailable, then you keep people at a hands distance from you.

2. You Have Insecurities

If you struggle to love yourself, then count it as a sign of emotional stress. People are likely to be unavailable emotionally for others when they are emotionally unavailable for themselves too. We always doubt the people who love us. How can they when I, myself, can't? And this self-hatred eventually results in a distant relationship with your fellow beings. Pampering yourself time by time is essential for every single one of us. It teaches us how one should be taken care of and how to support each other.

3. You Have A Terrible Past Experience

This could be one of the reasons for your unapproachable nature towards people. When you keep some terrible memory or trauma stored inside of you, it's most likely you cannot comfort some other being. It won't seem like something you would do. Because you keep this emotional difference, you become distant and are forced to live with those memories, making things worse. It would help if you talked things out. Either your parents or your friends. Tell them whatever is on your mind, and you will feel light at heart. Nothing can change the past once it's gone, but we can work on the future.

4. You Got Heartbroken

In most cases, people are not born with this nature to be emotionally unavailable. It often comes with heartbreak. If you had a breakup with your partner, that could affect your emotional life significantly. And if it was a long-term relationship, then you got emotionally deprived. But on the plus side, you got single again. Ready to choose from scratch. Instead, you look towards all the negative points of this breakup. Who knows, maybe you'll find someone better.

5. You Are An Introvert

Do you hate going to parties or gatherings? Does meeting with friends sound tiresome? If yes, then surprise, you are an introvert. Social life can be a mess sometimes. Sometimes we prefer a book to a person. That trait of ours makes us emotionally unavailable for others. It is not a bad thing to stay at home on a Friday night, but going out once in a while may be healthy for you. And the easiest way to do that is to make an extrovert friend. Then you won't need to make an effort. Everything will go smoothly.

6. You Hate Asking For Help

Do you feel so independent that you hate asking for help from others? Sometimes when we get support from others, we feel like they did a favor for us. So, instead of asking for help, we prefer to do everything alone, by ourselves. Asking for aid, from superior or inferior, is no big deal. Everyone needs help sometimes.

Conclusion

Being emotionally unavailable doesn't make you a wrong person, but being there for others gives us self-comfort too. It's not all bad to interact with others; instead, it's pretty fun if you try. It will make your life much easier, and you will have a lot of support too.

CPSIA information can be obtained
at www.ICGtesting.com
Printed in the USA
BVHW042256301121
622875BV00015B/775